The Steps

of a

Good Man

Dr. Thomasina A. Jones

ISBN 0-7414-5388-6

Unless otherwise indicated, Scripture quotations marked (NLT) are taken from the Holy Bible, New Living Translation, Copyright © 1996 by Tyndale Charitable Trust. All rights reserved.

Scripture quotations marked (NKJV) are taken from the New King James Version®. Copyright © 1982 by Thomas Nelson, Inc. Used by permission. All rights reserved.

Scripture quotations marked (NIV) are taken from the Holy Bible, New International Version®. NIV® Copyright© 1973, 1978, 1984 by International Bible Society. Used by permission of Zondervan. All rights reserved.

Scripture quotations marked (KJV) are from the King James Version of the Holy Bible.

Back cover photo credit: Dom's Photo Center, 41 S. Laurel Street, Bridgeton, NJ 08302

Published by:

INFI∞ITY
PUBLISHING.COM

1094 New DeHaven Street, Suite 100
West Conshohocken, PA 19428-2713
Info@buybooksontheweb.com
www.buybooksontheweb.com
Toll-free (877) BUY BOOK
Local Phone (610) 941-9999
Fax (610) 941-9959

Printed in the United States of America
Published May 2009

Dedication

To my husband and the five "Good Men" who worship with him every morning; I applaud you for being men whose steps are ordered by the Lord!

Acknowledgments

I am extremely grateful and indebted to a number of people who committed time and energy to help me along this breathtaking journey. I would like to acknowledge Ms. Brenda Jones who has been with me since the beginning; Ms. Arletha Lane, my copy editor, for her steadfast and untiring commitment to help me bring this project to fruition; and my Bishop, Dr. Keith W. Reed Sr., for his support and teaching me Biblical truth.

I am obliged to the Lord Jesus Christ for my husband Cris; sons Shawn, Cristopher, and Solomon; parents Thomas and Tina; sisters Darlene, Iesha and Deborah; brother Pastor Kato Brown; cousin Trish; Empowerment Hour women; and friends Tonya Richardson and Paula Riley, for their prayers, whispers of encouragement, shouts of victory, unwavering love, commitment and support as I completed another element of my journey.

Table of Contents

Preface

The topic of discussion among any group of women, single or married, young or old, rich or poor, will inevitably lead to a formidable, fiery and sometimes turbulent discussion about men. Although some women may deliberately attempt to avert the topic, someone within the confines of the group will ultimately divert the group to a dialogue about men.

The topics of debate range from men being Spiritual leaders, head of households, fathers, role models, lovers, providers, Casanovas, manipulators and warriors to good for nothing absent fathers.

Unfortunately, there is always at least one woman in the crowd who has had a negative experience with a man. It could have been a rocky relationship, a man who abandoned her, a father who failed to fulfill his financial obligations to his family, or countless other experiences. The women who have encountered a damaging relationship with a man have the propensity to use the one negative relationship as a barometer to measure the worth of all men.

Women who have been subjected to harmful relationships with men are instrumental in leading their fellow sisters, friends and colleagues to believing that all men are tainted, worthless and useless.

Generally, when the topic of men and their destructive attributes are exhaustibly discussed, there is a common strand that resounds and resonates in the minds and hearts of women. Where are the good men? We have heard the saying, "A good man is hard to find." A Good Man is not so hard to find if one knows one when she encounters one. There are certain characteristics, virtues, qualities, morals and values that a Good Man constantly demonstrates and exemplifies. The quandary is that some women are unaware and oblivious of the unique characteristics of a Good Man.

The title of this book "The Steps of a Good Man" originates from Psalm 37. God in His infinite wisdom and power has clearly delineated in His word the attributes of a Good Man. Psalm 37:23 (KJV), *"The steps of a good man are ordered by the Lord, and he delighteth in his way."*

A Good Man is a person, whom God delights, follows God, trusts Him, has hidden the word of God in his heart and seeks to do the will of the Father. As a result, God guards over every step he takes along the journey. *"The law of his God is in his heart; none of his steps shall slide."* Psalm 37:31 (KJV)

Women no longer have to ask the question, "Where are the good men?" Women who are tuned to the word and voice of God, coupled with possessing the Spirit of discernment, will undoubtedly readily identify the steps of a Good Man.

Chapter One

A Good Man is Hard to Find

It was that time of year again. The time to convene in a quaint, intimate restaurant with a group of single and married, stunning, intelligent women to discuss mundane topics such as careers, hobbies, families, educational journeys and church ministries. The conversation originated with everyone taking the round robin approach to discuss the topics at hand. Suddenly, without any warning, one of the single women emerged with a pervasive topic no one was prepared to thrash out. She started talking about her urgent desire to be married. It was a topic that thousands of women have discussed over the years.

None of the women were astonished at the topic because everyone had previously heard it from a family member, friend or colleague. The women were bewildered that she was having an arduous time connecting with a potential mate. She was an attractive, smart, dazzling female who possessed the attributes of a phenomenal woman. They could not fathom why it was getting increasingly difficult for their friend to pinpoint a Good Man.

The women stared into their friend's eyes and poignantly asked why she was having a difficult time discovering the right man. The friend gazed into the eyes of the women and stated, "I am having difficulties ascertaining a mate because a Good Man is hard to find!" Several of the single women immediately sanctioned and corroborated her position. Fortunately, one of the blissfully married women interjected and asserted that there were some Good Men in the world. Her single, frustrated friend rhetorically responded that she needed to relocate to another planet because she had not been auspicious enough to meet any Good Men on earth!

The married woman thought the single woman expressed an inscrutable response that had infiltrated the hearts of women seated around the table. She lamented over the perilous comments and generalizations that were being made about men. She immediately refuted their innuendos, took an imperturbable stance, elevated her voice, and declared that there were Good Men on earth. She avowed that women must be keenly aware of the distinct attributes and characteristics that are manifested and displayed by Good Men. The women movingly summoned their married friend to affirm the qualities of a Good Man which prompted her to give a written account of the attributes and characteristics of a Good Man.

Chapter Two

A Good Man Loves God

"Jesus said unto him, Thou shalt love the Lord thy God with all thy heart, and with all thy soul, and with all thy mind."

Matthew 22:37 (KJV)

Today, if you visit most church sanctuaries on Sunday morning, Bible Study classes during the week, or Sunday school, you will find that churches are predominately composed of women. It appears that women out number men by at least 2:1 in churches throughout the country. Women have assumed roles in the church that were at one time reserved for men. Women are often solicited to assume leadership roles in the church because men are unavailable to fill the positions. The United States of America 2006 Census data purports there are currently 151,963,645 women above the age of 18 residing in the United States in comparison to 147,434,940 men. The Census report clearly indicates that women supersede the number of men in the United States.

While women out number men in the United States, that is not solely the reason why so many men are absent from Sunday morning worship services, Bible Study and

Sunday school classes. There are litanies of reasons that men offer for being exempt from church-related activities. Men have stated they do not have time to attend church or Sunday school because the services and class times conflict with their prescheduled hobbies on Sunday. The church schedule may clash with golf, football, hockey, soccer, basketball, fishing, or any other hobbies they participate in on Sundays. They may not attend Bible Study during the week because it interferes with their work schedules or their favorite television shows. Scan some churches in America on Super Bowl Sunday and you will find a scant population of men in the sanctuary.

Another reason men have given for being absent from church is that they know everything they need to know about God; therefore, they do not need to attend church services or Bible-related classes to learn about God.

Although men have a vast number of reasons for not attending church activities, one of the most prominent reasons why men do not attend church is because they do not love the Lord with all of their hearts, souls and minds. The most vital attribute of a Good Man is that he loves God with all of his heart, soul and mind. Albeit church attendance alone does not necessarily constitute that a man loves the Lord with all of his heart, soul and mind, it is something that can be used as a barometer to measure a man's level of commitment to his relationship with God.

I have heard men say when they decide to settle down and get married they want to marry a "church girl." Men will abruptly place their hobbies on hold to visit sanctuaries on Sundays to pursue possible mates for marriage. Men literally seek potential wives in the church because they are looking for moral, upright women who love God. Men are astute enough to know they have a better chance at locating wholesome women in the church than in the local bar. They will ferociously search for women who sing on the choir, usher, teach and even preach because it increases their chances of finding someone who is not being pretentious about their relationship with the Lord.

Surprisingly, there are women who establish equivalent standards when seeking a candidate for marriage. They desire a good church man who has a relationship with God. Women who are considering a prospective mate should not only focus on church attendance but, ultimately concentrate on the man's personal relationship with God. The love of God with one's heart, soul and mind is the ultimate measure of a Good Man.

"Jesus said unto him, Thou shalt love the Lord thy God with all thy heart ..."
Matthew 22:37 (KJV)

Love is defined as a passionate affection for another person based on personal or familial ties; humankind's

7

dedication to or adoration of God. It is evident throughout the Holy Bible that God has an intense affection for mankind. *"Greater love hath no man than this, that a man lay down his life for his friends."* John 15:13 (NIV)

God has declared, demonstrated and exemplified the greatest act of unwavering and sacrificial love by *"sending Christ to die for us while we were still sinners."* Romans 5:8 (NLT) A Good Man recognizes the unfailing and incomprehensible love that God has for him and seeks to actively and earnestly express adoration towards God.

God commands men to *"love the Lord thy God with all thine heart, and with all thy soul, and with all thy might."* Deuteronomy 6:5 (KJV) *A* Good Man expresses his love towards God with his holistic being.

A Good Man loves God with his whole heart. The heart is the seat of one's affections. The heart has been defined as the most personal, intimate center of the natural condition of man. A Good Man has love and affection for God in the innermost receptacle of his heart. If a man loves the Lord with all of his heart, his behavior will manifest and reflect what is reverberating in his heart. A Good Man is one who loves God and has a heart that is devoted and committed to exalting, praising, reverencing and worshipping God.

I am fortunate because I attend church where men are not reluctant to convey their love and adoration towards the Lord. I have witnessed men serving the Lord with gladness, singing the praises of the Lord, publicly praying, waving their hands, crying and telling others about the goodness of the Lord. A Good Man is not averse to publicly or privately sharing his adoration, fondness and devoutness towards God. A Good Man is not reticent to lift up his voice in praise to state: *"The Lord is my strength and my shield; my heart trusted in him; and I am helped therefore, my heart greatly rejoiceth, and with my song will I praise him."* Psalm 28:7 (KJV)

One of the things that a woman should look for in a man is the condition of his heart. The Prophet Jeremiah posed a poignant question about the condition of a man's heart. He asked, *"The heart is deceitful above all things, and desperately wicked; who can know it?"* Jeremiah 17:9 (KJV) Thousands of women get entrenched in obstinate, negative relationships because they select mates who have hearts that are far away from God. There are some women who perceive men as being heartless and emotionless beings whose main focus is to manipulate and toy with the sentiments of women. They are the men who some women keenly describe as Casanovas and players.

I had a conversation with a woman who zealously declared that all men were awful, ruthless and immoral beings. I implored her to share the information that prompted her to make an egregious and volatile generalization about men. Unhappily, she suffered through several damaging experiences with men. She was able to present a chronological report of her harmful associations with the opposite sex.

I was flabbergasted to uncover that her pessimistic view of men originated with a college experience. The guy she dated in college cheated on her and subsequently, she continued to connect with players who concentrated on fulfilling their sexual desires by being with several women. She surmised that all men were foul and despicable beings because of her negative bouts with them.

The problem with her premise is that not all men are abominable, wicked, emotionless beings who sleep around with a litany of women. Although she may have experienced some negative relationships with men, generalizations should not be made about all men. There are some Good Men who recognize that seeking to satisfy sinful desires, and toying with the hearts of women, are contrary to the word of God and will ultimately impact every aspect of their lives.

Proverbs 4:23 (NLT) avows that, *"Above all else, guard your hearts, for it affects everything you do."* A Good Man comprehends that the heart embodies his emotions and feelings, so, he will not seek to carry out desires of his heart that are not congruent with God's principles. He will have a yearning need to deny his own desires because the love of God and his aim to please Him will prevent him from acting on sinful desires.

"Jesus said unto him, Thou shalt love the Lord thy God … and with all thy soul …"

Matthew 22:37 (KJV)

I have always been in awe and amazed by God's fearfully and wonderfully created masterpiece—man! *"And the Lord God formed man of the dust of the ground, and breathed into his nostrils the breath of life; and man became a living soul."* Genesis 2:7 (KJV) I marvel at the fact that God created man, who did not become a living soul, until a majestic, glorious and holy God breathed life into him!

The soul of a man is defined as "the individual's essential self, life, of being." (NLT Dictionary) God is the creator and originator of life. A man's life is a gift from God and his life and worth comes from God's Spirit. A Good Man loves God who is the maker of his life, and reverences Him with the innermost being of his soul.

"Jesus said unto him, Thou shalt love the Lord thy God … and with all thy mind."
Matthew 22:37 (KJV)

A Good Man loves the Lord with his entire mind. The mind is the part of man that engages in conscious thinking, feeling, and decision making. The heart and mind are akin to each other.

One day, I received a visit from a woman who was traumatized and hysterically wailing because she had uncovered that her husband was having an extramarital affair. She could not fathom that her husband would engage

11

in an act of betrayal and deceitfulness. She affirmed that she had done everything right as a wife. How could he do something so evil, contemptible and revolting to her? It was evident that her husband had allowed sin to enter into his heart. Once he failed to confess and repent for his sins, he started thinking about the act and the feeling of being with another woman. He allowed the act of adultery to fester and play over and over again in his mind until he made the conscious decision (in his mind) to commit infidelity.

I learned a long time ago that men are visual people. Married men (and single men) have to be extra careful not to get enticed by flirtatious, captivating women with striking physiques. Men must be cognizant that the act of adultery originates in the heart and then enters the mind. A Good Man is reminded of God's word that states: *"Casting down imaginations and every high thing that exalteth itself against the knowledge of God, and bringing into captivity every thought to the obedience of Christ."* II Corinthians 10:5 (KJV) A Good Man is going to *"be renewed in the spirit of his mind"* and abstain from deliberately participating in sinful activity. Ephesians 4:23 (KJV)

Proverbs 24:9 (KJV) declares that, *"The thought of foolishness is sin, and the scoffer is an abomination to men."* A Good Man recognizes that certain thoughts, feelings and decisions are simply foolishness and should not be brought to fruition. He has a satirical understanding that God understands his thoughts afar off and constantly bombards the throne of grace by declaring, *"Examine me, O Lord, and prove me; test my heart and my mind."* Psalm 26:2 (KJV) A Good Man who falters will ultimately say, *"I thought about my ways, and turned my feet to your testimonies."* Psalm 119: 59 (KJV)

A Good Man's converted soul enables him to turn away from sin and walk uprightly before the Lord. Women who seek to commit to a man should assess whether or not the man has affirmed his untiring and undying love for God. Women should ask men the question, "Do you love the Lord thy God with all thy heart, and with all thy soul and with all thy mind?" If the response is no, flee in the other direction!

Chapter Three

A Good Man Exemplifies the Fruit of the Spirit

"But the fruit of the Spirit is love, joy, peace, long-suffering, gentleness, goodness, faith, meekness, temperance ..."

Galatians 5:22-23 (KJV)

There was a young lady who was presumably dating a Good Man. She noticed that he attended church and his conversation suggested he loved God. He was involved in church and people appeared to gravitate towards his outgoing personality. The young lady was so deeply impressed with his testimony of love for God, his charisma and persona that she eventually married him. Shortly after the wedding ceremony, she noticed that he had become very controlling. He was condescending and often emotionally abusive. She was amazed at her husband's remarkable ability to alter his character to suit himself. She swiftly realized that she had married a Dr. Jekyll and Mr. Hyde!

There are some women who do not spend enough time and energy getting to know the core of a man's character before deciding to get intimately involved with him. I strongly believe there are red flags men display that should signal to a woman that the man is not who he purports to be. The quandary is women have the proclivity to blatantly ignore the signs. The young lady who suddenly uncovered that her new husband was controlling and abusive obviously was oblivious to that same controlling and abusive behavior while they were courting.

It is not enough for a man to declare and proclaim that he loves the Lord with all of his heart, soul and mind. He must be able to produce some fruit reflecting that the Spirit of Christ is dominant and preeminent in his life.

It is vital that men allow the Spirit of Christ to rule and reign in their lives. In the book of Galatians, Paul eloquently instructs Christians to, *"live by the Spirit, and you will not gratify the desires of the sinful nature. For the sinful nature desires what is contrary to the Spirit and the Spirit what is contrary to the sinful nature. They are in conflict with each other, so that you do not do what you want."* Galatians 5:16-17 (NIV)

There is a war going on between the Holy Spirit and the flesh (sinful nature). Men who do not allow the Holy Spirit to rule over their lives will produce the following outcomes: *"When you follow the desires of your sinful nature, your lives will produce these evil results: sexual immorality, impure thoughts, eagerness for lustful pleasure, idolatry, participation in demonic activities, hostility, quarreling, jealousy, outbursts of anger, selfish ambition, divisions, the feeling that everyone is wrong except those in your own*

15

group, envy, drunkenness, wild parties, and other kinds of sin ... " Galatians 5:19-21 (NLT)

A Good Man recognizes the need for a Holy Savior to empower him by the Holy Spirit to crucify his flesh (sinful nature) in order for him to manifest the fruit of the Spirit. A man who allows the Holy Spirit to control his life will exhibit the fruit of the Spirit. Galatians 5:22-23 (NIV): *"But the fruit of the Spirit is love, joy, peace, long-suffering, gentleness, goodness, faith, meekness, and self-control ... "*

"But the fruit of the Spirit is love ... "

The first virtue of the fruit of the Spirit is love. The term love is flippantly and superficially used in society. Sorry to say, some people do not have a clear and accurate understanding of the word love because it has become convoluted over the years. There are some men who have a distorted and warped understanding of love based on their relationships with people. There are men who tell women they love them when in fact it is lust masqueraded by love. Thousands of women have been duped and succumbed to relationships that were established on a foundation of lust and sex.

There was a young lady who came across a young man at a club. She was so thrilled. Finally an attractive man donned in a suit and tie appeared to be flirting with her. She

16

was spellbound because men did not usually approach her. The men normally loomed and gravitated towards her friends. The good-looking, charming, handsome man made his way over to her in the club. He immediately captivated her attention by telling her how she was the most beautiful woman in the club. He eventually solicited her for her phone number.

She dated him for two weeks and suddenly found herself in bed with him. She fervently believed that he adored and loved her. That prompted her to make "love" to him. Regrettably, the young lady discovered that the young man did not love her when he failed to return any of her calls after she made "love" to him!

There are four Greek words that define the word love. 1) *Eros* is a love that is carnal and sexual. 2) *Phileo* love is a brotherly love reserved for close friends and is where the term brotherly love originates. 3) *Storge* is love for family affiliations. 4) *Agape* love is the greatest form of love that is unconditional and seeks to serve others.

Eros love ...

The young lady was a recipient of an eros type of love which had a devastating effect on her life. She did not realize the young man had based their shallow relationship on an eros type of love that was laced with lust and sex. Thousands of women are manipulated by men to participate in eros-driven love affairs. Women are often confounded when they discover their lives have been ravaged and wrecked by men who were simply seeking to fulfill their sinful sexual desires.

Phileo and Storge love …

My mother always told me, "when seeking a man to marry, assess and observe how he treats his family, especially how he treats his mother." I have heard numerous stories from women regarding their love affairs with men and the families who reared them.

Beverly decided to settle down and marry a man who she met in college. She realized that Robert very seldom mentioned his mother or father. Quite frankly, she never heard him mention his sisters and brothers. She was amazed at his lack of discussion or interest surrounding his family because she was intricately involved with every fiber of her family's being. She had a stellar relationship with her father and was extremely close to her mother. She conferred with her siblings regarding career options, relationships and extracurricular activities. She did not make any decisions without deliberating with her parents or siblings.

Beverly noticed that during their college experience; Robert never went home to visit his family and friends. During the holidays, he spent time with her relatives. She became inquisitive and inquired about his relationship with his parents and siblings. He informed her that he was not close to his parents or siblings. He did not give her a definitive reason why he did not commune or sup with his family. Beverly did not ask any additional questions about his family until it was time to compose the guest list for their wedding. Beverly was astounded when Robert did not record the names of any family or friends on his wedding list!

Beverly did not have a barometer to measure if Robert exhibited phileo, a brotherly type of love that was reserved for family or friends. She never surveyed his relationship towards his family or friends because she was not afforded the opportunity to interact or mingle with them. It also was unmistakable that Robert did not depict a storge type of love towards his family because Beverly did not have an opportunity to observe Robert in familial settings with his relatives.

After a few years of marriage, Beverly realized Robert intentionally moved her and their children to another state to isolate her from family and friends. She was unfamiliar and oblivious to the following scripture which would have helped her decide if Robert had an accurate understanding of the word love: *"Love is not jealous or boastful or proud or rude. Love does not demand its own way."* 1 Corinthians 13:4-5 (NLT)

It is essential that women have the opportunity to observe men when they are in the company of their family and friends. Sadly, Beverly was taken by surprise when she discovered that Robert had an estranged relationship with his family.

On the other hand, Sharon was an intuitive, clever woman who had an astute understanding of the severity of appraising a potential mate's relationship with his family and friends. She intentionally orchestrated events that afforded her the opportunity to observe John in settings with his relatives and friends.

Sharon insisted that she meet John's parents once she was interested in him. She met his father and mother at a dinner engagement. She found that his parents were both God-fearing people. Both of his parents were officers in their church and they had a high regard for each other. She noticed how they assisted each other in the kitchen with the meal they prepared for her, John and his siblings.

John's siblings honored and revered him because he was an exceptional brother. It was evident that they looked up to their big brother and sought his advice regarding any decisions that had to be made in their lives.

During the visit, everyone laughed and enjoyed each other's company. John's parents showed Sharon the family photo album that included family vacations, baby and college photos.

Sharon was impressed with John's family. Upon the conclusion of the family dinner, she surveyed how John and his siblings pitched in to help by cleaning off the table, placing the dishes in the dishwasher and taking the trash out while his parents served her coffee. As the family exited the home, everyone kissed, embraced and stated, "I love you."

Phileo love ...

Sharon was not a sports fan but she accompanied John when asked to attend a football game with a group of his friends. She carefully examined John's interactions with his friends. He was very courteous and polite towards his friends. He offered to organize the trip and drive to the stadium. He dropped everyone off at the gate so they did not have to take the long hike to the stadium. During the game, some of the guys had some discussions about the performance of the football team. They were respectful of each other's views and opinions.

After the game, John embraced all of his friends and thanked them for sacrificing the time to fellowship with the group. Sharon studied how John interacted with his friends and also how much his friends valued his comradeship. Sharon evaluated John's bond with his family and friends and was immediately reminded of 1 Corinthians 13:4 (NIV): *"Love is patient, love is kind."*

There are some men who exhibit and manifest Eros, phileo and storge expressions of love; however, the love that

God is referring to in I Corinthians 13:13 (NJKV) is the greatest form of love. *"And now abide faith, hope, love, these three; but the greatest of these is love."* Agape love is the form of love all men should seek to demonstrate in their relationships with others.

Agape love ...

Jesus is the perfect example of agape love. Agape love is the greatest form of love that is unconditional, friendly, loving and seeks to serve others. John 3:16 (NLT), *"We know what real love is because Christ gave his life for us. And so we also ought to give up our lives for our Christian brothers and sisters."*

A Good Man seeks to attain the highest form of love. The kind of love that God indwells Good Men with is affectionate, unselfish, demonstrative and directed towards others. It is impossible to manifest and exhibit agape love without the love of Christ ruling and abounding in a man's heart. A man that loves God with his heart, soul and mind; demonstrates agape love for fellow man; and seeks to fulfill the needs of others by denying himself are characteristics of a Good Man. John 13:34-35 (NLT), *"A new command I give you: Love one another. As I have loved you, so you must love another. By this all men will know that you are my disciples, if you love one another."*

"But the fruit of the Spirit is joy ..."

I was recently watching an episode on television about several individuals that had committed suicide by jumping off of one of the most infamous bridges in the United States of America. There was a common denominator amongst all of the men who had committed suicide. They were unhappy with the current state of their lives. I immediately thought of the women who were left behind as a result of their decisions to abruptly end their lives. Were they able to unequivocally detect that the men in their lives were so despondent and dejected that they were contemplating suicide?

The Greek word for joy is chara which means joy, rejoicing, gladness, enjoyment and bliss. A Good Man will possess the second fruit of the Spirit, joy. Authentic joy that echoes in the heart of man is richer than happiness and is deeply rooted in knowing that God's presence dwells within him. The joy that David is referring to is not based on a man's current circumstances. It is based on the presence of Christ residing with man. Psalm 16:11 (NLT), *"You will show me the way of life, granting me the joy of your presence and the pleasures of living with you forever."*

It is fundamental for women to be acquainted with the state of a man's heart. A man who has the presence of God in his heart will be joyful and enjoyable to be around because; his joy is not based on the external conditions that surround him.

It is necessary for a man to know the distinct difference between happiness and joy. Happiness that is based on emotions or situations can ultimately be disconcerting because circumstances, emotions and actions will change.

A Good Man has a keen understanding that he acquires his joy from not only knowing God, but also by being cognizant that he will live with God forever. A Good Man will be joyful and content in his current state because he realizes that God will never leave him nor forsake him.

A woman seeking to pinpoint a Good Man must examine the man's character when he is experiencing duress. Does he remain joyful and blissful when he is experiencing some friction or discomfort? Does he immediately become depressed and reclusive when things are not going according to his plans? Does he have an optimistic outlook on life in spite of the uncertainties that surround him? It is vital that a woman be knowledgeable about whether or not a man has joy before she commits to a relationship with him. A man that lacks joy can abruptly abandon her if the complexities of life triumph over him.

"But the fruit of the Spirit is peace ..."

Peace "Shalom" is defined as tranquility, harmony, free of strife or discord. A man manifesting the fruit of the Spirit (peace) will exhibit signs of the peace he has with God, in his relationships with others, and in the community. A man that lacks peace, due to a nonexistent relationship with God, will experience disharmony in his relationships and in the community.

Spiritual Peace

Romans 5:1 (NLT), *"Therefore, since we have been made right in God's sight by faith, we have peace with God because of what Jesus Christ our Lord has done for us."*

The ultimate form of peace is for man to have a harmonic relationship with God. A man attains peace with God when He accepts Jesus Christ as his personal Savior. Jesus Christ paid the fundamental price for man's sin when He died on the cross. Any man that loves the Lord with all of his heart, soul and mind is no longer separated from God because of sin. After a man has been reconciled unto God, God endows him with His peace. *"The Lord will give strength to his people. The Lord will bless His people with peace."* Psalm 20:11 (NLT)

The relationship between God and a Good Man is free from dissension, discord, contention and hostility because the peace of God dwells in the heart of the Good Man. Job 22:21 (NKJV), *"Now acquaint yourself with Him, and be at peace; thereby good will come to you."* A Good Man will experience Spiritual peace that can only be bequeathed to him by God when he seeks after God with his heart, soul and mind.

Peaceful Relationships

II Corinthians 13:11 (NLT), *"Dear brothers and sisters, I close my letter with these last words: Rejoice. Change your ways. Encourage each other. Live in harmony and in peace. Then the God of love and peace will be with you."*

A Good Man will have the inward peace of God which will be outwardly exemplified in his relationships with others. A man that has a personal encounter with Jesus Christ should be the author and progenitor of peace and not strife. The peace of God that dwells in a man should be evident in his life and manifested in his daily interactions and relationships with mankind. A man that is consistently involved in contemptuous relationships with others is not allowing the fruit of the Spirit called peace to be eminent in his life.

Bill (in his 30s) had a hazardous and volatile relationship with his family. He resided with his father, mother and brother. He would often speak ill of his family members in front of people. Bill would constantly be at the center of arguments that occurred in the home. He caused so much strife in the household that his parents literally dreaded being around him.

Bill's parents did not feel comfortable ousting him from the home, henceforth; they allowed him to continue to reside with them. Bill continued to perpetuate an environment of acrimony and hostility amongst his family. Ironically, Bill stated that he had a relationship with God.

Bill's parents and brother noticed that he was a church gypsy. He joined a new church every six to 12 months. He found something negative to say about the Pastor or one of the parishioners, and abruptly abandoned the church. Bill's family members could not uncover any wrongdoing on the part of the Pastor or the church parishioners. It appeared that Bill was always responsible for being the author of confusion. In I Corinthians 14:33 (KJV) Paul stated, *"for God is not the author of confusion but of peace!"*

Bill's mother and father allowed their 30-something-year-old son to remain in their residence because he could not maintain a job. Bill often obtained a job then suddenly had a conflict or quarrel with a colleague. He received termination notices due to his battles and disputes with his peers and superiors. Bill left the imprint of strife and discord amongst his family, friends and colleagues.

Bill's verbal proclamation of his inward relationship with God should have been noticeable and discernible. The word of God expressively states in Psalm 34:14 (KJV), *"Depart from evil, and do good; seek peace, and pursue it."*

A Good Man has inner peace with God that ultimately gives him the strength to have external, peaceful relationships with others. Psalm 29:11 (KJV), *"The Lord will give strength unto his people; the Lord will bless his people with peace."*

Peace within the Community

"If it be possible, as much as lieth in you, live peaceably with all men."

Romans 12:18 (KJV)

In 2007, Philadelphia was no longer identified as the city of brotherly love. It acquired the nickname "Killadelphia" due to the soaring number of citizens that were murdered in the city. The predominate gender of the slaughtered victims were men. Paradoxically, the repulsive homicides also were committed by men. What would cause someone to be so incensed and enraged that he would take the life of another human being?

It appeared that a vast number of the slayings in Philadelphia occurred because of conflicts and disputes that occurred amid people in the community. In some instances, innocent bystanders were shot and killed due to feuds that originated with members of the community. The Bible states in Proverbs 20:3 (NLT), *"Avoiding a fight is a mark of honor; only fools insist on quarreling."* A Good Man has the internal peace of God which transcends to peaceful relationships with members of the community.

Matthew 5:9 (KJV) states, *"Blessed are the peacemakers; for they shall see God."* A Good Man will work towards establishing harmonious, serene and unified relationships with people in the neighborhood, community, job, church and nation. Men, who declare to have a personal relationship with Jesus Christ, and the indwelling of His Holy Spirit, should not be the originator or nucleus of battles that occur within their communities. A respectable man will seek diplomacy and peace with his fellow men. He will attempt to encourage, educate, instruct and build up his fellow man in order to improve his life.

A noble man recognizes that he will not always be in synchrony with the ideals, beliefs and values that members of his community hold. He is mindful of the word of God, and adheres to Romans 12:18 (NLT), *"Do your part to live in peace with everyone, as much as possible."* A Good Man will be the conduit for peace in his community by holding up the banner of Shalom and ensuring that he is holding fast to the word of God and the profession of his faith. God promises in Proverbs 16:7 (KJV), *"When a man's ways pleases the Lord, he maketh his enemies to be at peace with him."*

"But the fruit of the Spirit is love, joy, peace, long-suffering, gentleness, goodness, faith, meekness, temperance ..."

Galatians 5:22-23 (KJV)

Jesus is the greatest example to mankind of one who is love and exhibits love, compassion and longsuffering towards men. God exemplifies his untiring, unfailing love and patience towards men in spite of the sin they commit. God's tireless love, longsuffering, forgiveness, kindness and devotion should not prompt men to freely and haphazardly indulge in sin. *"Well, then, should we keep on sinning so that God can show us more and more kindness and forgiveness? Of course not! Since we have died to sin, how can we continue to live in it?"* Romans 6:1-2 (NLT) The inexorable love that God demonstrates towards men, should enable men to exhibit longsuffering to the people they interact with on a daily basis.

The Greek word makrothumia means longsuffering, patience and forbearance. A Good Man will embody the attributes of Christ and manifest patience and self-restraint when he encounters difficult, dishonorable, mean-spirited people along the journey. He will be less apt to sever relationships with people, or cast them aside as a result of sinful action committed towards him.

There is an incredible, mind-boggling, warm hearted man in the Bible that experienced great adversity. In spite of the hard times he faced, he exhibited and demonstrated the fruit of the spirit. Joseph was someone who loved God and willingly manifested the fruit of the spirit despite the egregious acts that were displayed towards him. Joseph's story is extremely unique and by far is an example of a Good Man who demonstrated the fruit of the spirit (longsuffering, gentleness, goodness, faith, meekness and temperance, or self-control) towards people who were cruel, malicious and wicked.

Joseph was the son of Rachel and Jacob. Rachel had religiously prayed for a child after being barren for many years. Joseph was special to his father, Jacob, because he was born to him at an elderly age and he exemplified stupendous character. Joseph's brothers were extremely jealous of him because they were keenly aware that their father favored their brother. They became enraged when their father presented their youngest brother with an extravagant robe that was generally worn by lavishly rich people. Genesis 37:4 (NLT), *"But his brothers hated Joseph because of their father's partiality. They could not say a kind word to him."* Genesis 37:5-9 (NLT), *"One night, Joseph had a dream and promptly reported the details to his brothers, causing them to hate him even more. 'Listen to this dream,' he announced. 'We were out in the field tying up bundles of grain. My bundle stood up, and then your bundles all gathered around and bowed low before it!' 'So you are going to be our king, are you?' his brothers taunted. And they hated him all the more for his dream and what he had said. Then Joseph had another dream and told his brothers about it. 'Listen to this dream,' he said. 'The sun, moon, and the stars bowed low before me!'"* Joseph's brothers became extremely agitated, frustrated, and enraged by his dreams.

Joseph's siblings were infuriated and troubled by his apparent boastful behavior. They were so incensed by his conduct that they conspired to murder him! *"When Joseph's brothers saw him coming, they recognized him in the distance and made plans to kill him. Here comes that dreamer! they exclaimed. Come on, let's kill him and throw him into a deep pit. We can tell our father that a wild animal has eaten him. Then we'll see what becomes of all his dreams!"* Genesis 37:18-20 (NLT)

Fortunately, Reuben decided to rescue his brother by offering his brothers an option. He convinced them not to kill Joseph but to place him in the pit. Reuben presumed he would later return to a pit to retrieve his brother. Unfortunately, when Reuben left the scene of the crime, his brothers decided to change the agenda. They collaborated and decided to sell Joseph into slavery instead.

Joseph's brothers were so conniving they told their father that their brother was dead. The brothers had taken Joseph's extravagant robe and dipped it in blood to convince Jacob that his son was killed by a ferocious animal.

Joseph was an upright man whom God loved. After being sold into slavery, Joseph was purchased by Potiphar, a member of Pharaoh's staff, and captain of the palace guard.

Potiphar noticed that Joseph was favored by the Lord and placed him in charge of his house and business.

One day while Joseph was in the quarters, Potiphar's wife summoned Joseph to sleep with her. Joseph being a godly man did not accept her invitation. Potiphar's wife was so angry he turned down her request that she conjured up false sexual allegations against him. Joseph was imprisoned by Potiphar because he believed his wife's allegations. *"But the Lord was with Joseph there, too, and he granted Joseph favor with the chief jailer."* Genesis 39:21 (NLT) The chief jailer, like Potiphar, placed Joseph in charge of the entire prison!

God favored Joseph and eventually made him ruler over Egypt. He settled down in Egypt, married and fathered two sons. His sons' names were Manasseh—God has made me forget all my troubles and the family of my father; and Ephraim—God has made me fruitful in this land of my suffering.

After seven years of prosperity, there was a famine in the land of Egypt and Canaan. Joseph had storehouses full of grain; therefore, he was able to provide grain to others. Astoundingly, Joseph's brothers came to Egypt and petitioned him to buy grain! They did not recognize Joseph; however, he instantly recognized them. Joseph provided his family with the grain they needed to survive.

Ultimately, Joseph did not blame his brothers for selling him into slavery. He stated, *"I am Joseph, your*

brother, whom you sold into Egypt. But don't be angry with
yourselves that you did this to me, for God did it. He sent me
here ahead of you to preserve your lives. God has sent me
here to keep you and your families alive so that you will
become a great nation. Yes it was God that sent me here, not
you!" Genesis 46:4-5, 7-8 (NLT)

Joseph was afflicted by the hatred, pain and ruthless
acts from the people closest to him—his brothers! He was
able to show the longsuffering spirit that he manifested by
accepting the plan that God had for his life. He did not
complain when his brothers placed him in the pit, separated
him from his father, or sold him into slavery. He did not
protest when he was placed in jail, or whine about how he
was falsely accused of a crime.

It was apparent that Joseph displayed gentleness and
goodness towards his siblings in spite of their harsh
treatment towards him. During the famine, Joseph was
concerned about the welfare of his family. In Genesis 42:25
(NLT), Joseph demonstrated an act of gentleness and
kindness towards his brothers. *"Joseph then ordered his*
servants to fill the men's (brothers) sacks with grain, but he
also gave secret instructions to return each brother's
payment at the top of his sack. He also gave them provisions
for their journey." Joseph refrained from holding a grudge
against his siblings but offered gentleness and kindness when
they needed him most.

Joseph noticeably had faith in God. He was able to translate dreams that were given by God, interpret them, and watch the dreams come to fruition. Genesis 41:25 (NLT), *" 'Both dreams mean the same thing,' Joseph told Pharaoh. 'God was telling you what he is about to do.'"* Genesis 41:39 (NLT) reflects that others had faith in Joseph's visible trust in God. *"Turning to Joseph, Pharaoh said, 'Since God has revealed the meaning of the dreams to you, you are the wisest man in the land!'"*

Joseph was a meek and humble man of God. He was a recipient of God's favor. Joseph held several admirable positions as a result of the favor God had given him with others. The favor and blessings Joseph received from God were transcended to the people who surrounded him. Genesis 40: 5 (NLT) stated, *"From the day Joseph was put in charge, the Lord began to bless Potiphar for Joseph's sake."*

Joseph was submissive to God and gentle in all of his leadership roles. He was especially meek when he did not allow his brothers' offenses, or transgressions to hinder him from accepting them into his household. *"Weeping with joy, he (Joseph) embraced Benjamin, and Benjamin also began to weep. Then Joseph kissed each of his brothers and wept over them, and then they began talking freely with them."* Genesis 45:14-15 (NLT)

It was clear that Joseph demonstrated every attribute of the fruit of the Spirit including self-control. During the time that Joseph served Potiphar, he was propositioned by

Potiphar's wife to indulge in sexual immorality. Joseph's relationship with God and the respect he had for Potiphar was more important than sexual gratification. Joseph's response was, *"'Look,' he told her, 'my master trusts me with everything in his entire household. No one here has more authority than I do! He has held back nothing from me except you, because you are his wife. How could I ever do such a wicked thing? It would be a great sin against God.'"* Genesis 39:8-9 (NLT)

Joseph was an awesome man of God. Potiphar, the Chief jailer, Pharaoh, his brothers and the people of Egypt and surrounding countries recognized that God was with Joseph. Men whose steps are ordered by the Lord are readily identified by others. Although Pharaoh and his staff were pagans, they recognized Joseph as a God fearing, great and remarkable man of God. Genesis 41:38 (NLT), *"As they discussed who should be appointed for the job, Pharaoh said, 'Who could do it better than Joseph? For he is a man who is obviously filled with the spirit of God.'"* Joseph exemplified longsuffering, gentleness, goodness, faith, meekness, and self-control because the Spirit of God was with him!

Chapter Four

A Good Man is Wise

"Listen, my son, accept what I say, and the years of your life will be many. I guide you in the way of wisdom and, lead you along the straight paths. When you walk, your steps will not be hampered; when you run, you will not stumble. Hold on to instruction, do not let go; guard it well, for it is your life."

Proverbs 4:10-13 (NIV)

Mary was infuriated with her husband, Jim. They had taken a road trip to visit his sister in Pennsylvania. The estimated arrival time to Jim's sister's house was two hours. Mary instructed her husband to take a road map; however, Jim assured her that he was familiar with the route. It became apparent, after the road trip lasted in excess of three hours, that Jim was lost.

Mary kept insisting that Jim stop at a gas station to ask for directions. Jim ignored his wife's request and continued to drive aimlessly around the state of Pennsylvania. Jim was adamant that he knew how to get to his sister's house; therefore, he proceeded to drive in spite of his wife's fervent plea to seek assistance from a gas station attendant, or to purchase a map from one of the many convenience stores they encountered along their journey. Unfortunately, Mary and Jim never made it to his sister's house. Jim finally gave up after taking an eight-hour excursion across the state of Pennsylvania!

There were several things that Jim could have done to prevent his incredible eight-hour trek. Jim should have listened to his wife and accepted her help. Mary told Jim to take a road map with him on the outing. The road map would have given Jim the directions and guidance he needed to help him reach his destination. The atlas would have assisted Jim in reaching his goal with minimal detours, hindrances, roadblocks and obstacles. Jim would have arrived at his sister's house free of any impediments or obstructions if he had simply studied the road map, placed it in his vehicle and frequently referred to it during his travels. The map would have given Jim the information he needed to lead him on a direct path to his sister's house!

There are a lot of men in the world that exhibit Jim's attitude and conduct. They fail to listen to God, accept His direction, seek His guidance, and study His Bible in order to be prepared for life's journey. A Good Man recognizes that he needs the wisdom of God to successfully navigate through the issues of life.

James 1:5 (NIV) states, *"If any one of you lacks wisdom, he should ask God, who gives generously to all without finding fault, and it will be given to him."* Some men are reluctant to ask for directions. A man that loves God with all of his heart, soul and mind will not be ashamed to seek God for direction or understanding. Because his desire is to please God, he will learn about the principles of God's word.

Johnny was employed as an administrator. His job required that he travel throughout three contiguous states. One of Johnny's family members endowed him with one of the best gifts he had ever received—a navigation system! Johnny was extremely ecstatic about the vast and remarkable benefits the navigation system afforded him. First, after he input the address of the destination, the navigation system offered him specific directions to his target. Second, the navigation system recalibrated and changed Johnny's direction if he encountered any detours or roadblocks along his route. Third, the navigation system included a database of roads in the entire country. Johnny was mesmerized that the navigation system had the ability to provide him with a map of every area of his impending journeys!

The Bible is the gift that God has given man to enable him to obtain the wisdom he will need to navigate through the trials and tribulations of life. A Good Man is wise and seeks to embrace and cling to God's wisdom because he realizes that without it, he would stagger, stumble and falter along his journey. *"Happy is the person who finds wisdom and gains understanding. For the profit of wisdom is better than silver, and her wages are better than gold. Wisdom is more precious than rubies; nothing you desire can compare with her. She offers you life in her right hand, and riches and honor in her left. She will guide you down delightful paths; all her ways are satisfying. Wisdom is a tree of life to those who embrace her; happy are those who hold her tightly."* Proverbs 3:13-18 (NLT)

A Good Man is vigilant about acquiring knowledge of God. He is studious about spending quality time learning about the principles and precepts of God's word in order to find out the blueprint that God has for effective living. He comprehends and understands that without knowledge of God, he would make foolish decisions and fail to carry out the principles of God's word.

A Good Man hides the knowledge he has attained from God in his heart. During the time of trouble and distress, he will make sound judgments and choices based on the instruction he has acquired from God and will apply it to every aspect of his life.

Joseph was a wise man who was favored by God. Joseph's in-depth familiarity and experience with God afforded him the opportunity to maintain his posture as a man of God when he encountered some inequities, turbulence, suffering, and distress along the journey. Proverbs 24:5 (KJV) states, *"A wise man is strong, yes, a man of knowledge increaseth strength."* Joseph's understanding of God, his awareness of the circumstances around him, and having the know-how to navigate through the situations he encountered along his journey deem him a wise man.

A Wise Man Listens to Advice ...

"Fools think they need no advice, but the wise listen to others."

Proverbs 12:15 (NLT)

The Lord blessed Joseph with the uncanny ability and gift to interpret dreams. As a teenager, he told his dreams in details to his father and brothers. His brothers snickered at his dreams and simply called him a dreamer; however, his father listened and kept the matter in mind. Upon being sold into slavery and jailed, Joseph continued to interpret dreams. People (including Pharaoh's cup-bearer and baker) recognized that Joseph was in tune with God; therefore, they trusted him to decode their dreams and accepted his advice. *"'I had a dream last night,' Pharaoh told him, 'and none of these men can tell me what it means. But I have heard that you can interpret dreams, and that is why I have called you.' 'It is beyond my power to do this,' Joseph replied, 'But God will tell you what it means and will set you at ease.'"* Genesis 41:15-16 (NLT)

Joseph interpreted the dreams for Pharaoh. *"Joseph's suggestions were well received by Pharaoh and his advisers. Turning to Joseph, Pharaoh said, 'Since God has revealed the meaning of the dreams to you, you are the wisest man in the land! And Pharaoh said to Joseph, I hereby put you in charge of the entire land of Egypt.'"* Genesis 41:37, 39, 41 (NLT)

Pharaoh recognized that he and his advisers had some difficulties accurately interpreting the dreams. He was astute enough to seek the advice of someone endowed with knowledge which could only come from the true and living God. It was evident that Pharaoh listened to the advice of Joseph when he acted on his counsel and planned for the impending prosperity and famine of Egypt.

A Wise Man Does the Right Thing ...

"Doing wrong is fun for a fool, while wise conduct is a pleasure to the wise."
Proverbs 10:23 (NLT)

Dave and his wife Melissa were married for over 25 years. Dave was employed in an environment that predominately consisted of women. There was a young, charming and good-looking woman who was definitely attracted to Dave. Susan deliberately pursued Dave in spite of his well-known marital status. She was the first person Dave encountered at the water cooler in the morning. She calculatingly wore provocative apparel in order to captivate Dave's attention. Susan complimented Dave on his attire, level of intelligence, sense of humor and physique. As Susan walked away from Dave, he watched her sashay down the hallway. Dave sensed that something was not right about Susan; however, he enjoyed spending time with her. He repetitively told himself the conversations at the water cooler were not iniquitous and that he could handle his relationship with Susan.

One day Susan asked Dave to join her for lunch at a local restaurant. Dave convinced himself it would be a harmless lunch rendezvous. Unfortunately, what was supposed to be an innocuous lunch date eventually escalated into a full blown extra marital affair! Dave could have avoided the entrapment of a seductive woman if he simply used wisdom!

In the embryonic stage of Dave and Susan's relationship, Dave perceived something was wrong. Instead of Dave doing the right thing, using wisdom and acknowledging that the relationship was immoral, he knowingly delved into a relationship with Susan. As a result of the extramarital affair, Dave's wife divorced him; his family abandoned him, he lost all of his assets, and Susan moved on to the next guy in line at the water cooler! *"But a man who commits adultery lacks judgment; whoever does so destroys himself."* Proverbs 6:32 (NIV)

Yet again, I am reminded of Joseph. He was a wise man who did the right thing. He was also hunted and tracked by a provocative and seductive woman. He used good judgment and did not succumb to her vile and sinful devices. *"And about this time, Potiphar's wife began to desire him and invited him to sleep with her. But Joseph refused ... She kept putting pressure on him day after day, but he refused to sleep with her, and he kept out of her way as much as possible."* Genesis 39: 7-10 (NLT)

Joseph's main concern was his relationship with God. He had God's favor upon his life. If Joseph had obliged Potiphar's wife, it would have been a great sin against God. Joseph was not willing to let a manipulating, revolting, woman hinder his relationship with almighty God. Joseph's knowledge of God, favor with God, relationship with God, and desire to live upright for God, afforded him the opportunity to be abundantly blessed by God. Joseph was blameless, highly favored by God and had an impeccable record as a wise leader because he focused on doing the right thing.

Chapter Five

A Good Man Has Integrity

"The integrity of the upright will guide them, but the perversity of the unfaithful will destroy them."

Proverbs 11:3 (KJV)

"Good people are guided by their honesty; treacherous people are destroyed by their dishonesty."

Proverbs 11:3 (NLT)

One complaint that women often have about men is their lack of integrity. Women have a yearning desire to interact with honest, upright, complete, moral, and law abiding men. Unfortunately, some women have encountered men who were dishonest, liars, thieves and cheaters. Oftentimes, scores of men engage in immoral and vicious activities that destroy them and the women they love. Women from various cultures, ethnicities, economic, educational, professional and religious backgrounds have been emotionally shattered by men who lack integrity. The women who unite with men lacking integrity recognize that the dishonest, deceitful and decadent behavior ultimately wreck their lives.

A small town daily newspaper in the Northeast area reported that, a local investment broker bilked $1.3 million from a group of elderly people. The authorities alleged, the broker told investors he had special bonds which would offer them an annual return rate of 6 and 11 percent. The scheme used investors' money to perpetuate itself, and it fell apart because there was no actual business behind it. The perpetrator used the money to pay for his children's private schools, mortgage, lavish cars, jewelry, in-ground swimming pool and extravagant clothing. It was evident that the investment broker lacked integrity!

The wife believed that her husband's business was trustworthy, lucrative and prosperous. She had no knowledge that her husband was a devious man with a fraudulent business. After the FBI presented her with the charges, she immediately realized her husband was not the honorable, upright man she thought she married. The man she loved and the father of her four children had defrauded a group of senior citizens out of their life savings.

The investment broker's fraudulent practices reflected how deceitful and vile he was. Apparently, he had a strong desire to uphold a standard of living that he could not honestly afford. Proverbs 28:6 (NLT) states, *"It is better to be poor and honest than rich and crooked."* The investment broker was not a righteous man who adhered to tenets of God's word. The Bible clearly states: *"The trustworthy will get a rich reward, but the person who wants to get rich quick will only get into trouble."* Proverbs 28:20 (NLT) Regrettably, the woman the investment broker married, and the children he fathered, were destroyed as a result of his crooked scheme.

There was an episode on one of the popular news magazine shows concerning a man who brutally attacked four people. The FBI was baffled by the perpetrator's ability to remove all DNA and fingerprint evidence from the crime scene. The FBI's profile of the perpetrator reported it was presumably someone who was in law enforcement.

After a thorough investigation, and a frantic call from a woman who heard a man attempting to break in her home, the police had a suspect in custody. The FBI's profile of the suspect was accurate. The perpetrator was a police officer! He was a decorated officer with 17 years experience on the police force. The attacker was a married man with two teenaged daughters, who served as a coach for one of the community athletic teams.

Despite the FBI informing his wife of all charges, the witnesses' identification of the assailant in a line up, DNA evidence found on a mask in his garage and a conviction from a jury, his wife stood by her husband and fervently believed he was innocent. Her defense was that the man she married had integrity and would not commit such a heinous crime.

Sadly, there are some women who refuse to accept the truth about the men they love in spite of the evidence presented to them. There are red flags, signs and concrete evidence which supports that the men in their lives lack integrity. Unfortunately, they are unjust but the women continue to love them and make excuses for their wrongdoing. God expects men to live just lives, and He expects women to hold men to His standard of right living. Women who unite with men who are unjust must expect God to discipline and hold the men they love accountable for their actions. Men should anticipate God's correction when they participate in pursuits that are depraved, wicked and destructive.

A young lady married a guy who appeared to be a Good Man. During the course of the marriage, she uncovered that her husband owed the Internal Revenue Service a debt. He had the propensity to claim a high number of dependants on his taxes in order to have a greater take home pay. One day, an astute IRS representative became suspicious and audited the man. His wife was shocked. Her husband owed the IRS a whopping $20,000! She was absolutely furious! She always paid her taxes and abided by the laws of the land. She became entangled in her husband's web of deceit. She had not realized her husband lacked integrity until after she united with him in marriage.

There are immeasurable stories that women have told about men who lack integrity. One of the overarching complaints many women have about men, as it relates to integrity, is a man's inability to be in an honest, purely monogamous relationship. Numerous women have been emotionally destroyed by men because they uncovered that their men cheated on them. Men have gotten tagged as Casanovas and players because of the women who have been scorned by them.

I was scrolling through the channels one day and noticed a new reality television show. I became inquisitive about the title of the show and decided to watch an episode. I was astonished to uncover that the show was about men and women who cheat on their spouses! I want to make it clear. Not all of the couples on the show were married people; however, there were a vast number of people who were married.

Quite frankly, I found the show to be appalling. If a woman or man suspected that his or her spouse was cheating, he or she contacted the producers of the show. The producers of the show sent out a team of people to conduct surveillance of the person accused of infidelity. The hidden cameras recorded the man or woman engaged in the affair. The producers shared a video tape recording of the husband and mistress with the wife. The wife had an emotional breakdown after viewing the recording.

After the wife recovered, the producers placed her in a vehicle and drove her to a location where she could face her husband in the presence of the mistress. Imagine the adrenaline, the emotional rollercoaster, the lies and the betrayal the wife experienced as she confronted her husband.

The wife's world was turned upside down when she realized the man she married was a cheat and lacked integrity.

It is critical that women look for the red flags that would suggest the men in their lives may not be walking in integrity. Little "white lies" men tell should not be overlooked.

Men who tell lies may also cheat on the women they proclaim to love. A man who is comfortable calling his employer and telling him he is home sick with the flu when in fact he is going to a baseball game lacks integrity. The same man may also call the woman he is supposedly in a serious relationship with to tell her that he has to work late when in fact he has a date with another woman. A man that is inspired by the word of God recognizes that *"an honest witness tells the truth; a false witness tells lies."* Proverbs 12:17 (NLT) A Good Man is an honest man that will always tell the truth!

It is fundamental that women study and scrutinize the character of men to detect if they possess integrity. Proverbs 20:7 (NKJV) states: *"the righteous man walks in integrity."* Men who possess integrity will walk in honor, truth and righteousness. A blameless man abhors participating in activities that are dishonest and impure for he realizes immoral endeavors will lead him on the road to destruction.

A Good Man devoted to God has steps that are ordered by the Lord. He will walk upright before God and the people he proclaims to love. His feet will be firmly placed on the principles and precepts of God's word. He will walk in integrity, always seeking the Lord to examine his ways to ensure that his actions are congruent with God's word. A Good Man's mantra is, *"Judge me, O Lord; for I have walked in mine integrity: I have trusted also in the Lord; therefore I shall not slide. Examine me, O Lord, and prove me; try my reins and my heart. I have walked in my truth!"* Psalm 26:1-3 (KJV)

Chapter Six

A Good Man Has a Vision

"Where there is no vision, the people perish: but he that keepeth the law, happy is he."
Proverbs 29:18 (KJV)

There was a couple who reared their children in the fear and admonition of the Lord. They religiously took their children to worship services, Sunday school, Bible Study and youth ministry activities. The parents prayed with their children, read the scriptures to them, and taught them the precepts and principles of the Holy Bible. The parents instilled in their children the importance of acquiring knowledge of God and communing and listening to God in order to fulfill the vision God had for their lives.

Sadly, the parents noticed that one of their sons started to engage in behavior that was contrary to the Godly instruction he was taught. The son was no longer adhering to his parents' authority and guidance. He became disobedient, defiant and noncompliant to any of the instructions his parents outlined for him. The parents extended correction; however, he combated and rebutted their correction. The son eventually engaged in criminal activities which landed him in a correctional facility. *"When people do not accept divine guidance, they run wild. But whoever obeys the law is happy."* Proverbs 29:18 (NLT)

The parents were devastated that their son was a resident of the penal institution. They had mapped out the journey their son would take in life. They made the expectations clear to him by frequently sharing the vision with him. The plan was for him to remain steadfast in the faith, go to college, attain a lucrative job, purchase his own home, marry and have children. Their son was clearly aware of the vision. They communicated it to him to prevent him from floundering during his journey.

How could a son allow outside influences to inhibit him from attaining the vision his parents outlined for him? What were the obstacles or hurdles that prohibited his vision from coming to fruition? The parents concluded that when their son stopped communing with God, and adhering to their instruction, his vision became clouded. He could no longer visualize the plan that God had for his life.

Jacob, like a lot of men, experienced some strife before he was able to attain the vision God had for his life. Jacob had a critical role in the plan which God created to develop a nation from the lineage of Abraham. Abraham, Isaac and Jacob were three of the most significant and influential people in the Old Testament. God selected them to fulfill His plan in spite of their individual weaknesses. They were cognizant of God's laws and, for the most part, lived by them.

Jacob, the son of Isaac and Rebekah and twin brother of Esau, experienced some hurdles in life. First, he grabbed his brother's (Esau) heel at birth. Second, he stole the birthright and blessing designed for Esau. In spite of the early problems Jacob had in terms of his deceitfulness, God loved and utilized Jacob to accomplish His plan. Jacob would eventually become the father of the 12 tribes of Israel: "A*t the top of the stairway stood the Lord, and he said, 'I am the Lord, the God of your grandfather Abraham and Isaac. The ground you are lying on belongs to you. I will give it to you and your descendants. Your descendants will be as numerous as the dust of the earth! They will cover the land from the east to the west and the north to the south. All of the families of the earth will be blessed through you and your descendants. What's more, I will be with you, and I will protect you wherever you go. I will someday bring you safely back to this land. I will be with you constantly until I have finished giving you everything I have promised.' ...Then Jacob made a vow: 'If God will be with me and protect me on this journey and give me food and clothing, and if he will bring me back safely to my father, then I will make the Lord my God.'"* Genesis 28:13-15, 20 (NLT)

Jacob was able to confidently journey through life because he was keenly aware that the vision God revealed to him would be fulfilled. *"God said to Jacob, 'Now move on to Bethel and settle there.' ...God appeared to Jacob once again when he arrived at Bethel after traveling from Paddan-aram. God blessed him and said, 'Your name is no longer Jacob; you will now be called Israel.' Then God said, 'I am Almighty. Multiply and fill the earth! Become a great nation, even many nations. And I will pass on to you the land I gave to Abraham and Isaac. Yes, I will give it to you and your descendants.'"* Genesis 35:1, 9-12 (NLT)

A Good Man has knowledge about the vision God has for his life and pursues it until it comes to fruition. A man should be able to articulate the vision God has for his life and manifest evidence that he is working towards attaining the vision.

There are too many men being tossed to and fro because they have not learned of God, communed with Him, followed His guidelines, and tended to the revealed plan for their lives; therefore, they perish. In Genesis chapter 49 Jacob blesses each one of his 12 sons by sharing the vision for each one of their lives prior to his death. *"Then Jacob called his sons and said: Gather around so I can tell you what will happen to you in days to come."* Genesis 49:1 (NLT) Just as Jacob communicated the visionary blueprint to his sons, God has also given His children a clear understanding of the vision for their lives. Jeremiah 29:11-13 (NIV), *"For I know the plans that I have for you, declares the Lord, plans to prosper you and not harm you, plans to give you a hope and a future. Then you will call upon me and come pray to me, and I will listen to you. You will seek me and find me when you seek me with your whole heart."*

The young man's parents had given their son the instruction and expectations that God had for his life. Sorry to say, he like so many other men, discount and disregard the visionary design that God has for their lives. As a result of being unaware of God's revelation, they like the young man who refused his parents' direction, perish or are held in captivity!

Chapter Seven

A Good Man is a Good Husband

"And you husbands must love your wives with the same love Christ showed the church. He gave up his life for her."

Ephesians 5:25 (NLT)

Susan met the man of her dreams. He was educated, tall, handsome and financially secure. He came from an extremely large close knit family. His parents had been married for over 40 years and exemplified an intact family unit. Susan eventually embarked upon a relationship with Daniel which led to a serious courtship.

Susan was so excited. After two years of courting, Daniel popped the question and asked for her hand in marriage. She happily accepted and immediately started planning for the most important day of her life. Without delay, Susan contacted her friends and implored them to serve as bridesmaids. She located a church, wedding coordinator, caterer, reception hall, photographer and florist while she waited for the most important day of her life to arrive.

It was a beautiful, sunny, sultry day in June. Her husband had paved the way for her to have the best day of her life. He sent a white carriage with two beautiful white horses to pick up his wife at the door of the penthouse he had reserved for her bridal party the night before the wedding. She excitedly exited the penthouse and boarded the carriage drawn ride to meet her Knight in Shining Armor as well as 350 wedding guests. The Cinderella wedding appeared to be the happiest day of the bride's life. Sadly, Susan and Daniel's marriage ended in divorce three years later!

Most people, like Jesus, have been invited to witness a man and woman exchange marriage vows. *"On the third day a wedding took place at Cana in Galilee. Jesus' mother was there, and Jesus and his disciples had also been invited to the wedding."* John 2:1-2 (NIV) People attend weddings to witness the couple express their undying love and commitment to one another. Although Jesus had a divine purpose and plan for being at the wedding in Cana; marriage is honorable and worthy of a celebration with family and friends.

Unfortunately, more than 50 percent of marriages in the United States of America end in divorce. After all of the planning, preparation, money, romance, love and devotion, someone will plead irreconcilable differences warrant a divorce. The couples who participate in divorce court represent every ethnicity, socioeconomic background, religion, and age group. There are a multitude of people who have thrown in the towel and given up on the most sacred institution God has ordained, marriage.

There are people who filed for divorce and stated the reason for the severed relationship was irreconcilable differences. The two people agreeing to love honor and cherish one another failed to agree on certain issues, which invoked grounds for a divorce. It is imperative that people who contemplate marriage adhere to God's instruction for marriage before they utter their vows before God, family and friends.

In the book of Ephesians, Paul eloquently outlined the instructions for marriage. *"And further, you will submit to one another out of reverence for Christ. You wives will submit to your husbands as you do to the Lord. For a husband is the head of his wife as Christ is the head of his body, the church; he gave his life to her Savior. As the church submits to Christ, so you wives must submit to your husbands in everything. And you husbands must love your wives with the same love Christ showed the church. He gave up his life for her."* Ephesians 5:21-25 (NLT)

Paul made it crystal clear that married people must have a relationship with Jesus Christ and have a high regard for Him. During the courtship, it is vital to identify a potential spouse's relationship with God. A person who fails to show respect, commitment, devotion and submission to God will undoubtedly experience difficulty submitting to his or her mate.

The word submission has been sadly abused by so many people that women frown and recoil when the word submission is mentioned. In the book of Ephesians, the word Hupotasso—submit—is a Greek word that means to yield, be under or subject to one another. Jesus Christ, an almighty God, subjected Himself to the will and instruction of His Father. He submitted to God (the Father's authority) when He died on the cross! If a most holy, infallible and righteous God could submit unto God the Father, married people should be able to yield to one another.

Women must have a clear understanding of the expectations of marriage before they commit to marriage. God expects married women to subject themselves to His authority and the authority He has given to their husbands. *"You wives will submit to your husbands as you do the Lord."* Ephesians 5:22 (NLT) Most women do not have reservations or trepidation about submitting to the Lord. The mere fact that Paul expressed the need for wives to submit to the Lord and their husbands in the same sentence suggests the gravity of the expectation that God has for wives. Women who refuse to yield or subject themselves unto their husbands certainly are out of the will of God and are undeniably setting the stage for marital problems.

Paul powerfully recorded that God had given husbands the authority to lead and be the head of their households. Paul equated the function of husbands with the function and responsibility Jesus Christ has to the church. The scriptures reflect that Christ loved the church and gave His life for the church. 1 John 4:14 (NLT), *"Furthermore, we have seen with our own eyes and now testify that the Father sent his Son to be the Savior of the world. All who proclaim that Jesus is the Son of God have God living in them, and they live in God."* God mandates that women subject and yield themselves to their husbands in the same way the church submits unto the authority of Jesus Christ.

There are countless women who love God, and follow His Biblical blueprint. However; they wrestle with submitting to their husbands. There are women who are reticent to yield to, or obey a husband who demonstrates he is incapable of being the head of the household. Lamentably, too many husbands abdicate their responsibilities to their wives. The causation of women declining to submit to their husbands is because they have been forced to assume roles God designed for their husbands. The origin of some marital disputes is husbands who have failed to be competent in the roles, assignments and appointments God has given them.

Husbands have been instructed by God to love their wives as they love themselves. It is evident that a man who loves himself will take good care of himself and the people and things that are granted unto him. Unfortunately, some women have married men who do not have a clear understanding of their responsibilities as husbands.

I Timothy 5:8 (NLT), *"But those who won't care for their own relatives, especially those living in the same household, have denied what we believe. Such people are worse than unbelievers.*" One of the responsibilities of husbands is to financially provide for their families. There are a myriad of men who do not think it is their duty to be the providers for their families.

It would behoove all women to ask specific questions regarding a man's financial status during the courtship. Too many men have damaged credit reports, insurmountable debt, and in some cases, are not gainfully employed by choice. There are men who prefer not to work because the right job, in the right field, with the right salary, has not become available to them. Proverbs 12:22 (NIT) states, *"Hard work means prosperity; only fools idle away their time."* The women who choose to marry men who are financially destitute will find themselves having to work several jobs in order to maintain the household.

God did not intend married women to be the sole financial providers of their homes when they have husbands who are healthy and able to work. Husbands who decline to work to maintain their households, in God's view, are worse than infidels! Husbands who hand over their financial responsibilities to their wives may not have wives who are willing to yield to their authority because they do not respect their husbands.

Husbands have an obligation to cherish, honor and love their wives. Colossians 4:19 (NLT) states: *"and you husbands must love your wives and never treat them harshly."* The Lord expects husbands to love their wives just as he loved the church. God loved the church immensely. His love towards the church has been demonstrated in the lives of believers all across the world. There are numerous people who can testify to the love God exhibited towards them. Ultimately, God's perfect love was expressed towards men when he gave His life so, millions of believers across the world could be saved. John 15:13 (NIV), *"Greater love has no one than this that he lay down his life for his friends."*

God expects husbands to love their wives just as He loved the church. Husbands have a breathtaking responsibility. God did not state to love, honor and cherish her when things are going well. God loves the members of his church when they are not always loveable. He continues to express everlasting, unending and ceaseless love to His church when at times the love is not reciprocated.

Husbands are commanded to love their wives in spite of their shortcomings. God has given husbands the remarkable assignment of being the guiding leaders in the lives of their wives. It would be wise for husbands to look within themselves for answers regarding why their wives refuse to give in to their authority. Chances are the husbands have fallen short in terms of their responsibilities, if the wives are unwilling and oppose subjecting themselves to their husbands' authority.

Most women want to yield to and submit to their husbands. Wives are looking for righteous husbands who love the Lord and are obedient and subject to God's will and plan for their lives. Husbands will find that wives will readily submit and subject themselves to their authority if they are submitting to the authority, precepts and principles of God's word!

Chapter Eight

A Good Man is a Good Father

"And you, fathers, do not provoke your children to wrath, but bring them up in the training and admonition of the Lord."

Ephesians 6:4 (NKJV)

Donna had a prestigious position as an attorney in a prominent organization. She was humbled by her esteemed and influential position. One day, Donna shared some vital information about the person responsible for her success.

Donna was extremely fond and proud of her extraordinary father. It was her father's love, Godly instruction, encouragement, support, prayers, guidance and financial support that enabled her to attain her law degree.

Donna's father was employed as a blue collar worker. He was ecstatic when he received the news that his daughter was accepted to law school. Donna could not fathom how her family would financially be able to send her to college. Her father assured her he would find a way for her to attend law school. He was a Good Man and recognized that it was his responsibility to secure resources to send his daughter to college. Her father acquired a second job as a night custodian in order to fulfill his daughter's dream to become a lawyer. He worked 16 to 20 hours a day to pay her law school tuition.

One of the duties of the custodian was to check the status of the boiler. Her father had to journey down several flights of stairs to a dark and eerie basement to assess the boiler. During her father's trek to the basement, he was viciously attacked by a knife-wielding man. He suffered serious injury and was hospitalized for weeks.

Donna was adamant that her father needed to resign and relinquish his job as a night custodian because it was extremely dangerous. She told him she would withdraw from law school so that he did not need to work two jobs. Donna's father assured her he would be all right. He guaranteed her that he would bounce back from his injuries. Donna exited the hospital and decided to remain enrolled in law school due to her father's encouragement and support.

A couple of years after the brutal stabbing of her father, Donna graduated from law school and was preparing for the bar exam. She was exuding confidence until she received some disturbing news. Her father completed his night shift custodial work and was walking to his car when suddenly a masked gunman appeared out of nowhere. He robbed and shot Donna's father! Her father's vital organs were damaged as a result of the assault. Donna was furious and devastated that her father, her anchor, protector, provider and staunch supporter, had been victimized a second time. Donna sat at her father's bedside at the hospital. She prayed without ceasing for her father's healing. She quietly made a vow in her inner spirit, that she would not sit for the bar exam.

Several days later, Donna's father opened his eyes. She was present at his bedside. Donna immediately rejoiced and thanked the Lord for answered prayer. Her father was able to verbally communicate with his family. He immediately inquired about her bar exam. Donna attempted to tip-toe around the topic. Her father was very intuitive and right away suspected something was wrong. He questioned her a second time regarding the status of the bar exam. She delicately informed him that she was not going to sit for the bar exam because of her need to be with him. Her father used every ounce of strength he had to sit up in bed. He looked Donna in the face and emphatically told her he was not stabbed and shot for her to give up her dream to be an attorney. He told her he would be fine and there was no need to worry about him. He informed her she would be assisting him with his recovery if she proceeded to do what he always dreamt for his daughter—taking the bar and becoming an attorney.

A few weeks later, Donna sat for the bar exam and passed! Her father was able to witness the fruit of his labor. Her father was so proud of her accomplishments but more significantly, Donna was proud of her father. Donna was blessed because she had a father who provided her with the nurturing, guidance, support and instruction from God that she needed to be successful. Proverbs 4: 4 states: *"My father told me, take my words to heart. Follow my instructions and you will live."* Donna adhered to her father's instruction and as a result, she brought joy to her father.

Regrettably, Donna's father is not the norm in today's society. There are limitless children residing in homes across the United States of America in which their fathers do not live. The disintegration of the nuclear family is due to people opting to refrain from marriage, divorce, and out-of-wedlock births which have resulted in a mass number of children residing in fatherless homes. The mere fact that more than 50 percent of marriages end in divorce, coupled with an escalating number of out-of-wedlock births; leads to the distressing conclusion that most children will reside in a single parent home for a portion of their lives.

Despondently, fatherhood in the traditional sense is practically nonexistent because so many fathers do not reside with their biological children. Children who reside in homes in which their fathers do not live may be condemned to a life of poverty. Sadly, when fathers exit the homes where their children reside, they often take their financial assistance with them; forcing mothers to work several jobs to compensate for the loss of the father's financial backing. The dissolution of the nuclear family, predominately caused by the absence of a father, has had a profound impact on the children's well-being.

It is vital that fathers do not renounce their declaration from God to bring up their children in the fear and admonition of the Lord simply because the relationship with the mother has severed. Proverbs 1:8-9 (NLT) states: *"Listen, my child, to what your father teaches you. Don't neglect your mother's teaching. What you learn from them will crown you with grace and clothe you with honor."*

First, He instructs fathers to be leaders in assuring their children are taught the precepts and principles of God's word. Second, He instructs mothers to also teach their children. Regretfully, many fathers have abandoned their positions and handed over their responsibilities to mothers to train their children to respect, honor and love God and ultimately, be productive members of society.

In addition, too many children have not been afforded the opportunity to be crowned with grace and clothed with honor because their fathers have failed them by being selfish and caught up in their own lives. They happily surrender their children into the hands of people to provide them with life-saving instruction. Some fathers ardently believe that because they comply with child support orders outlined by the courts, they have done their duties as fathers. Albeit, providing financially resources to children is one of the roles of fathers, it is one of many responsibilities.

Sorrowfully, some fathers are unaware of the definition of fatherhood. The role of fathers is not just to plant a seed, but the role of fathers is to nourish, cultivate, offer guidance, support, care and love to their children. Historically, fathers assumed roles as nurturers, protectors, moral guides, teachers and primary breadwinners. Sadly, so many fathers have aborted their responsibilities which have contributed to some of the societal ills.

One of the reasons why more than 50 percent of children live in single parent headed households is due to divorce. Men who have severed relationships with the mothers of their children may cease contact with the children.

Men who father children should be instructing their children in the word of God. Instead of observing mothers carting children to churches on Sunday mornings, the fathers should be responsible for ensuring their children are in church and learning about God.

Men who have children should not allow their new wives, or girlfriends, to hinder or inhibit them from having an active, loving, relationship with their offspring. During the courting part of a relationship, if a man discovers that the woman refuses to love, nurture, cultivate and care for his children, then she should be avoided. Women who do not embrace the men's children will undoubtedly serve as a stumbling block and not a stepping stone in ensuring the children develop a personal relationship with God. Females who have personal relationships with God, and who are knowledgeable about God's word, ultimately recognize the expectations and responsibilities God has given to fathers.

They will encourage their husbands to train the children they fathered in the fear and admonition of the Lord.

Fathers who fail to properly care for their children will have to give an account to God. Ephesians 6:4 (NLT), *"And now a word to you fathers. Don't make your children angry by the way you treat them. Rather, bring them up with discipline and instruction approved by the Lord."* Children expect their fathers to offer them instruction and discipline. Children will become incredibly angry and bitter towards their fathers when they fail to do what is required of them.

Some fathers cannot fathom why their children have written them off as fathers. Fathers need to look in the mirror and ask themselves the following questions, "Have I been providing my children with Godly instruction? Am I contributing to the success or the demise of my children?"

Proverbs 4:10 (NLT), *"My child, listen to me and do as I say, and you will have a long, good life!"* Donna believed her father provided her with Godly instruction and as a result, she had a blessed life. She has a personal relationship with God, a wonderful husband and a successful career. She attributes her growth and development to both of her parents. However; her father adhered to God's instruction and trained her in the fear and admonition of the Lord. For that, she is most grateful!

Chapter Nine

A Good Man Leaves a Legacy

"Now therefore in the sight of all Israel, the assembly of the Lord, and in the hearing of our God, be careful to seek out all the commandments of the Lord your God, that you may possess this good land, and leave it as an inheritance for your children after you forever."

I Chronicles 28:8 (NJKV)

Countless people vividly and painfully recall where they were when they heard the alarming news on April 4, 1968. Dan Rather, a correspondent for CBS News, interrupted the local television shows to air a CBS News Special Report. Mr. Rather conveyed the news which devastated shocked and ravaged people across the United States of America. The CBS News correspondent stated, "The Reverend Martin Luther King Jr. was shot to death by an assassin late today as he stood on a balcony in Memphis, Tennessee." People all over the country were confounded and overwhelmed with the news announcing a Good Man, one of America's most fearless, prolific, and valiant Civil Rights leaders, was assassinated.

The night before Dr. King was gunned down he stood and gave his final awe-inspiring, magnificent, thought provoking speech at Mason Temple to approximately 2000 people. Some of those in attendance were most likely sanitation workers, politicians, city officials, grandparents, husbands, fathers, wives, children and members of his team. Most of the people in the audience came to hear the courageous and intrepid Dr. King share his plan to erase racial injustice, and racial discrimination against Black people.

Dr. King stood before the crowd and declared, "Well, I don't know what will happen now. We've got some difficult days ahead. But it doesn't matter with me now, because I've been to the mountaintop. And I don't mind. Like anybody, I would like to live a long life. Longevity has its place. But I am not concerned about that now. I just want to do God's will. And He's allowed me to go up to the mountain. And I've looked over. And I've seen the Promised Land. I may not get there with you. But I want you to know that tonight, that we, as a people; will get to the Promised Land. And I'm happy, tonight. I'm not worried about anything. I'm not fearing any man. My eyes have seen the glory of the coming of the Lord." The next evening, Dr. King was on the second floor balcony of the Lorraine Motel when he was hit by a sniper's bullet that killed him.

Millions of people were devastated by the abrupt and untimely death of Dr. King. The Civil Rights leader with a non-violent approach had been instrumental in leading non-violent movements, rallies, marches and boycotts to express disdain, dissatisfaction, and frustration with Jim Crow laws and unequal rights under the law for Black people. The people were distraught because someone killed their noteworthy and skilled leader; a person who would have led them to the Promised Land.

The citizens were so broken by the news; they did not realize that Dr. King had proclaimed his legacy unto them the night before his assassination. His speech had endowed them with the instruction, and plans they needed to get to the Promised Land!

King David, reminiscent of Dr. King, shared his legacy with the people and his son Solomon before his departure. David summoned a crowd of people to hear his declaration. The people in attendance were officers, commanders, officials, mighty men and brave warriors. King David rose to his feet and made the following speech to the people of Israel, *"Listen to me, my brothers and my people. I had it in my heart to build a house as a place of rest for the ark of the covenant of the Lord, for the footstool of our God, and I made plans to build it. But God said to me, 'You are not to build a house for my Name, because you are a warrior and have shed blood.' Yet the Lord, the God of Israel, chose me from my whole family to be king over Israel forever. He chose Judah as leader, and from the house of Judah he chose my family, and from my father's sons he was pleased to make me king over all Israel. Of all my sons—and the Lord has given me many—he has chose my son Solomon to sit on the throne of the kingdom of the Lord over Israel. He said to me: 'Solomon your son is the one who will build my house and my courts, for I have chosen him to be my son, and I will be his father. I will establish his kingdom forever if he is unswerving in carrying out my commands and laws, and is being done at this time.'"* 1 Chronicles 28: 2-6 (NIV) King David, like Dr. King, declared to the masses the instructions they required to fulfill the plans of God. Both Dr. King and King David were instrumental in leaving legacies for the nation to inherit and conquer after their departure.

As a part of King David's legacy, he left specific directions to the people of Israel and his son Solomon. *"So now I charge you in the sight of all Israel and of the assembly of the Lord, and in the hearing of our God: Be careful to follow all the commands of the Lord your God, that you may possess this good land and pass it on as an inheritance to your descendants forever. And you, son Solomon, acknowledge the God of your father, and serve him with whole-hearted devotion and with a willing mind, for the Lord searches every heart and understands every motive behind the thoughts. If you seek him, he will be found by you; but if you forsake him, he will reject you forever. Consider now, for the Lord has chosen you to build a temple as a sanctuary. Be strong and do the work. Then David gave his son Solomon the plans for the portico of the temple, its buildings, its storerooms, its upper parts, its inner rooms and the place of atonement."* I Chronicles 28:8-11 (NIV) King

David developed the blueprint the people and Solomon needed to carry on his legacy. The plan King David left would be the legacy a Good Man should follow in order to fulfill the promise God has for his life.

A legacy of adhering to the will of God....

There were three children that suddenly lost their father due to a heart condition. The children realized they no longer had a father to converse with regarding their life experiences. They also feared they would not be taken care of financially. His offspring thought they would not be able to identify the plans their father had for their lives due to his sudden departure. The children were startled to learn their father had outlined the plans for them via a will that was given to the executor of his estate.

The executor contacted the children and directed them to attend a meeting to hear the written contents of the will. The children were stunned because the will not only included a financial benefit; it included written plans for promoting and fostering a relationship with Jesus Christ, the importance of active prayer, college, relationships, family, marriage, childrearing and investing that would impact their lives. The children were instructed to adhere to the plans contained in the will or they would not be granted the items enclosed in it.

The children were thankful to their father for leaving them with the tools they needed to carry on his desire for each one of their lives. More importantly, the children believed the greatest gift their father left them was his guidance regarding a relationship with Jesus Christ. Likewise, God's will is simply that men should adhere to and follow the instructions and plans that God has conceived for them in the Bible.

Dr. King and King David both made it clear they wanted to do the will of God. Dr. King wasn't concerned about the things that could happen to him. His main concern was that he would do the will of God. King David told his son Solomon to acknowledge God, and serve Him whole-heartedly with a willing mind. It is imperative that men leave a legacy of the importance of adhering to the will of God. Both extraordinary men realized it was more important to do God's will than to fulfill their own selfish desires. *"I delight to do thy will, O my God, and your law is within my heart."* Psalm 40:8 (NKJV)

A legacy of adhering to God's commandments….

King David was committed to following the com-mandments of God. He directed his son to *"Be careful to follow all the commands of the Lord your God."* I Chronicles 28:8 (NKJV) Astoundingly, too many men do not ardently believe they have to follow God's commandments. God expects men to follow His commandments, remain committed to His word and as a result, they will be blessed. *"Now the days of David drew near that he should die, and he charged Solomon his son, saying: I go the way of all the earth; be strong, therefore, and prove yourself a man. And keep the charge of the Lord your God: to walk in His ways, to keep His statutes, His commandments, His judgments, and His testimonies, as it is written in the Law of Moses, that you may prosper in all that you do and wherever you turn; that the Lord may fulfill His word which He spoke concerning me, saying If your sons take heed to their way, to walk before Me in truth with all their heart and with all their soul, He said, you shall not* lack *a man on the throne of Israel."* 1 Kings 2:1-4 (NJKV)

Solomon learned how to adhere to the commandments of God by listening to his father endow him with God's plan for his life. Men who fail to grab hold of the principles of God's word place themselves in jeopardy of not receiving all of the great benefits God has for them.

A legacy of benefits….

Good Men leave legacies that ultimately benefit the lives of their children. Unhappily, there are litanies of men that leave legacies which do not benefit their children. The

Temptations wrote a song entitled, "Papa Was a Rolling Stone." Eventually he died and left his family alone. There are countless legacies of unfaithful husbands, ungodly men, deadbeat dads, absent fathers, men with bad credit, unemployed men, selfish men, and men with a history of criminal activity, etc. There are some children who have inherited legacies from their fathers that have caused them strife, grief, trouble and poverty. God promises to extend benefits and opulence to the children of men who honor His commandments.

God directed King David (a shepherd by trade and the Second King of Israel) to instruct his son Solomon to follow the precepts and principles of His word. If Solomon adhered to the conditions of God's word; he would receive some great benefits. *"Your son Solomon will build my Temple and courtyards, for I have chosen him as my son, and I will be his father. And if he continues to obey my commands and regulations as he does now, I will make his kingdom last forever. So now, with God as your witness, I give you this charge for all Israel, the Lord's assembly: Be careful to obey all the commands of the Lord your God, so that you may possess this good land and leave it to your children as a permanent inheritance."* 1 Chronicles 28:6-8 (NLT) Solomon was obedient to the will, and commandments of God. He built the temple as instructed by God's plan; and he received the benefits of God.

Solomon assembled the people, stood before them, and shared his account of the benefits he received from God for adhering to his commandments. He stated, *"Blessed be the Lord God of Israel, who spoke with His mouth to my father David, and with His hand has fulfilled it, saying, Since the day that I brought my people Israel out of Egypt, I have chosen no city from any tribe of Israel in which to build a house, that My name might be there; but I chose David to be over My people Israel. Now it was in the heart of my father David to build a temple for the name of the Lord God of Israel. But the Lord said to my father David, Whereas it was in your heart to build a temple for my name, you did well that it was in your heart. Nevertheless you shall not build the temple, but your son who will come from your body, he shall build the temple for my name. So the Lord has fulfilled His word which He spoke; and I have filled the position of my father David, and sit on the throne of Israel, as the Lord promised; and I have built a temple for the name of the Lord God of Israel."* 1 Kings 8:15-20 (NKJV)

The legacy King David left for his son Solomon had been fulfilled. Solomon was amenable to carrying out God's plan because he was accustomed to observing his father hold fast to the will and commandments of God. It was God's plan and King David's obedience to His commandments that caused Solomon to receive God's benefits. Solomon's benefits included serving as the third King of Israel, being known as the wisest man who ever lived and developing the kingdom of Israel to its greatest level of material wealth and land.

A Good Man leaves an inheritance for his children ...

"A good man leaves an inheritance to his children's children." Proverbs 13:22 (NKJV) It is essential that men leave an inheritance for their children which ultimately transcends to the lives of their children's children. Sadly, too many men depart earth failing to leave an inheritance for their children or grandchildren.

Oftentimes, men fail to prepare a will that includes a financial bequest, land, bonds, possessions or positions for their children and grandchildren to inherit. A myriad of children and grandchildren have inherited bills, funeral expenses and debt after the death of their fathers. Mothers and family members are found scurrying around seeking resources to make ends meet when the fathers depart without leaving a financial plan in tact for their children.

The lack of planning, preparation, investing, and saving prohibit children from receiving an inheritance from their fathers. God's expectation is that Good Men will leave a legacy for their children that include an inheritance.

King David instructed his son Solomon to adhere to the will, and commandments of God so that he would receive the benefits of God. Solomon not only received God's benefits for himself; his children received an inheritance from God. *"Blessed is the man who fears the Lord, who delights greatly in His commandments. His descendants will be mighty on earth; the generation of the upright will be blessed. Wealth and riches will be in his house, and his righteousness endures forever."* Proverbs 112:1-3 (NJKV) King David instructed Solomon to, *"Be careful to obey all the commands of the Lord your God, so that you may possess this good land and leave it to your children as a permanent inheritance."* 1 Chronicles 28:8 (NLT)

King David's obedience coupled with his son's submission to God resulted in Solomon's children receiving an inheritance. *"Solomon reigned in Jerusalem over all Israel forty years. Then Solomon rested with his fathers, and was buried in the City of David his father. And Rehoboam his son reigned in his place."* II Chronicles 9:30-31 (NKJV)

Dr. King and King David were notable and exceptional leaders who God had appointed to lead thousands of people out of oppression. Although God mightily used Dr. King and King David to accomplish His plan, it was God's design for both men to leave legacies that could be carried out by other people. God had used them to demonstrate and illustrate to people that it is fundamental to adhere to the will of God and keep God's commandments, in order to attain the benefits and inheritance for their people. As a result of their obedience and commitment to God, the people of God were richly blessed! Ultimately King David's son Solomon ruled as King of Israel while Dr. King was ultimately responsible for millions of Black people obtaining their civil and equal rights under the law.

Dr. King and King David were extraordinary examples of Good Men. It is essential that men leave valuable legacies for their children and the people they come in contact with. Like Dr. King, and King David, men ought to declare and proclaim their legacies to people before they depart. People will be more apt to pass the baton to the next generation if they have a clear understanding of the legacy.

Chapter Ten

A Good Man's Steps Are Ordered By the Lord

"The steps of a good man are ordered by the Lord, and He delights in his way. Though he fall, he shall not be utterly cast down; for the Lord upholds him with His hand."

Psalm 37:23-24 (NKJV)

Thousands of women have participated in tumultuous and volatile discussions about men. Disappointingly, men have received mean and depraved reports by women who have encountered a number of heartless and ruthless men along the journey. Albeit some men have participated in immoral activities which may be the reason why they were verbally attacked by women; for the most part, there are Good Men whom God has implanted upon the earth.

King David an intrepid and valiant leader and the second king of Israel left an extraordinary legacy to his son. For the most part, people can readily recall David's encounter with Bathsheba and the murder of Uriah. They may not recollect that David was a fearless leader and a man after God's own heart. Women must not annihilate or dismiss men God has deemed "good" because they may have stumbled along the journey.

There are men who are fearfully and wonderfully made by the master of the universe! Women must pause to recognize that the Good Men whom God has positioned in their lives are not faultless or perfect. There are upright men who have wholeheartedly decided to live for God in spite of their shortcomings. They have come to realize they are not flawless and may sometimes stumble. The men delight in knowing that because they love the Lord with all of their heart, soul and mind, and have committed their hearts to God; He will not cast them aside when they periodically stagger through life's journey. *"The law of the Lord is in his heart; none of his steps shall slide."* Psalm 37:31 (NKJV)

There are innumerable men who have stumbled upon hurdles and failures during their journeys. Fortunately, God knows the heart of every man. *"I the Lord, search the heart, I test the mind, Even to give every man according to his ways, according to the fruit of his doings."* Jeremiah 17:10 (NJKV) King David was a Good Man that experienced some triumphs and failures as he navigated through the voyage that God had designed for him. It is critical to review David's life story to understand the love, favor and devotion that God had towards him even though he stumbled along the journey.

David was the youngest of Jesse's (an Ephrathite from Bethlehem) eight children. David was widely known for his encounter with a giant named Goliath who was over nine feet tall! Goliath was an enormous bully who tormented the

Israelites. He repeatedly challenged and pestered the Israelites to rumble with him. One day Goliath roared to the Israelites, *"'Do you need a whole army to settle this? Choose someone to fight for you, and I will represent the Philistines. We will settle this dispute in single combat! If your man is able to kill me, then we will be your slaves. But if I kill him, you will be our slaves! I defy the armies of Israel! Send me a man who will fight with me!' When Saul and the Israelites heard this, they were terrified and deeply shaken."* 1 Samuel 17:8-11 (NLT)

David was a courageous young man. He heard a rumor that the King was offering a bounty of some sort for the person who would slay Goliath. David inquired about the reward for the extermination of Goliath. *"David talked to some others standing there to verify the report. 'What will a man get for killing this Philistine and putting an end to his abuse of Israel?' He asked them. 'Who is this pagan Philistine anyway, that he is allowed to defy the armies of the living God?'"* 1 Samuel 17:26 (NLT)

David was informed that the report was accurate. The person who killed the giant would receive a reward! David informed Saul that he wanted to fight the Philistine. Saul attempted to dissuade David from fighting Goliath because he was a boy. David persisted and prepared for the battle with Goliath.

Goliath walked out toward David with his shield bearer ahead of him, sneering in contempt at this ruddy-faced boy.

"'Am I a dog,' he bawled at David, *'that you come at me with a stick?' And he cursed David by the names of his gods. 'Come over here, and I'll give your flesh to the birds and wild animals!' Goliath yelled. David shouted in reply, 'You come to me with sword, spear and javelin, but I come to you in the name of the Lord Almighty—the God of the armies of Israel, whom you have defied. Today the Lord will conquer you, and I will kill you and cut off your head. And then I will give the dead bodies of your men to the birds and wild animals, and the whole world will know that there is a God in Israel! And everyone will know that the Lord does not need weapons to rescue his people. It is his battle, not ours. The Lord will give you to us!' As Goliath moved closer to attack, David quickly ran out to meet him. Reaching into his shepherd's bag and taking out a stone, he hurled it from his sling and hit the Philistine in the forehead. The stone sank in, and Goliath stumbled and fell face downward to the ground."* 1 Samuel 17:41-48 (NLT) David removed the sword from Goliath's sheath and cut off his head. David was a courageous young man whom the Lord used in a colossal and powerful way.

David was appointed King of Israel at the age of 30. The Lord selected him to lead his people. He reigned as King for a total of 40 years. Under the direction of King David, Israel reached notoriety. Imagine! Even King David, a Good Man, a bold and spirited leader, a man after God's own heart, stumbled during his walk as King of Israel.

Unfortunately, King David in all his greatness participated in an adulterous relationship with a woman named Bathsheba and strategically had her husband Uriah killed. *"Then Nathan said to David, 'You are that man! The Lord, the God of Israel, says I anointed you king of Israel and saved you from the power of Saul. I gave you this house and his wives and the kingdoms of Israel and Judah. And if that had not been enough, I would have given you much, much more. Why, then, have you despised the word of the Lord and done this horrible deed? For you have murdered Uriah and stolen his wife. From this time on, the sword will be a constant threat to your family, because you have despised me by taking Uriah's wife as your own. Because of what you have done, I, the Lord, will cause your own household to rebel against you. I will give your wives to another man, and he will go to bed with them in public view. You did it secretly, but I will do this to you openly in the sight of all Israel.' Then David confessed to Nathan, 'I have sinned against the Lord.' Nathan replied, 'Yes, but the Lord has forgiven you, and you won't die for this sin.'"* II Samuel 12:7-12 (NLT) King David could have crawled in a hole after the Lord sent Nathan, the prophet, to confront him about his sin. Thankfully, he recognized his sin and sought God's forgiveness. David cried out to the Lord. *"Have mercy upon me, O God ...Blot out my transgressions. Wash me thoroughly from my iniquity, and cleanse me from my sin ...Create in me a clean heart, O God, and renew a steadfast spirit within me."* Psalm 51 (NLT)

King David was a Good Man who served the Lord. He was not only the King of Israel but a shepherd, poet, and most importantly, he was from the lineage of Jesus Christ! King David, who again, was the apple of God's heart, was also an adulterer and murderer. Although King David engaged in sin, he was godly sorry and repentant for his wrongdoing. As a result of King David's sin, he received some consequences. Some of his children died and King David was not afforded the opportunity to build the temple. God appointed his son Solomon to build the temple.

Through David's sin, and receiving God's forgiveness, he learned about the forgiveness, power and love of God. God was aware of the condition of David's heart when David sought Him for repentance. David wrote in Psalm 51 verse 17 (NKJV), *"The sacrifices of God are a broken spirit, a broken and a contrite heart—these, O God, You will not despise."*

David's steps were ordered by God. King David consistently communed, prayed, and consulted with God before he stepped out to lead the people of Israel. He also acknowledged the magnitude of internalizing the word of God in his heart so that he would not sin against God. He was the author of the infamous pledge, *"Your word have I hidden in my heart that, I might not sin against you."* Psalm 119:11 (NKJV)

King David is a striking and significant example of God's forgiveness towards men when they sometimes fail to walk in His ways. Even though King David sinned, God did not utterly cast him down. He was a Good Man who had stumbled during the journey, but God allowed King David to continue to remain in his position as King of Israel.

There was a man who vividly remembered the day his father walked out on his mother and three siblings. He was 11-years-old when his father left them. He resented his father and thought he was a poor excuse for a man because he abandoned his family. His mother was a God-fearing woman who persistently prayed for her husband and children. While her husband did not regularly attend church, she made certain her sons regularly attended Sunday school and church.

Later, the father and mother divorced and he eventually married another woman. The sons despised and resented their father for marrying another woman. Although the father provided for his children financially, the children scorned him for deserting them and failing to rekindle the relationship with their mother.

A decade after the father ditched his children he committed his heart to the Lord. He proclaimed to his sons his unwavering and steadfast love for the Lord. He started to actively participate in his sons' lives and in the lives of his grandchildren. He occasionally attended church with his sons, and in return, his sons intermittently attended his place of worship.

Early one morning, the sons received some devastating news. Their father suddenly died at the age of 68 without any warning! During the father's home going service, people had breathtaking and magnificent things to say about him, including his children. Their father developed into a Good Man that had become a church deacon, a great father and awesome grandfather. He had served his community, and most importantly, shared Jesus Christ with his children, grandchildren and anyone he encountered along the journey. Several days after the home going service, the wife contacted the sons to notify them that their father left a will. He bequeathed an inheritance to each one of his children! The children were astonished and grateful to God for their father who had, in time, become a Good Man.

Chapter Eleven

Thank God for Good Men!

"I thank my God, making mention of you always in my prayers, hearing of your love and faith which you have toward the Lord Jesus and toward all the saints, that the sharing of your faith may become effective by the acknowledgement of every good thing which is in you in Christ Jesus. For we have great joy and consolation in your love, because the hearts of the saints have been refreshed by you, brother."

Philemon 1:4-7 (NKJV)

The single frustrated woman who posed the question "Where are the Good Men?" can rest assured there are Good Men who are located on planet earth! Sorry to say, but they are usually the men who are not at the forefront of discussions amongst groups of women. They are men who women deliberately abstain from discussing in groups. Too many women sit idly by and listen to their female counterparts draw attention to and underscore their negative encounters with men. Women who are blessed to have Good Men in their lives must not allow their comrades to bash and thump on all men.

Men and women alike are not perfect beings. All men and women are subject to sin. Fortunately, Good Men (like good women) strive to emulate the character of Jesus Christ and as a result, God delights in them. There are multitudes of Good Men who God takes pleasure in because they follow, obey and trust in Him. They are husbands, fathers, grandfathers, brothers, uncles, cousins, nephews, leaders, preachers, teachers, friends and colleagues. They do not appear on the local news or newspapers for their positive contributions to their families, churches, communities and society. Sadly, the activities of the men who are not united with the Lord steal the attention and limelight from Good Men who mirror and reflect the attributes of Jesus Christ.

Thankfully, there are many Good Men in the world! They love the Lord with all of their hearts, souls and minds. The word of God emanates and permeates in their hearts as evident by the fruit that is manifested in their lives. They are men who women can readily identify based on their steps being ordered by the Lord.

I am reminded of a group of men for whom I have the utmost respect. There are approximately six men of faith who rise every morning to convene for a 5:00 AM conference call worship experience. All of the men have a common bond ... their faith in the Lord Jesus Christ! The six men recognized at different stages of their lives the need for a Holy God to extend them His hand of grace, mercy and salvation.

The men start their day by offering up expressions of love, adoration, and praise to a loving and wise God. They petition God's throne on behalf of the needs of their families, church, communities, and world. They encourage each other through scriptures, prayer and praise.

The guys embody and signify the elements of Good Men. Their love for God and commitment to Him is evident in the things they do for their families, church, employers, and communities. It is clear they are wise men who have integrity. They share their visions for one another when they fellowship together. Their wives have deemed them good husbands and fathers. They have created a legacy of prayer, worship, praise and commitment to God for the people who reside with them. The Good Men are worthy of credit and recognition for their everlasting and endless commitment to the Lord.

Thank God that He denotes and delineates what every man needs to be deemed a Good Man. Men (and women alike) must realize that, having the spirit of God residing and resonating in one's heart, adhering to the word of God, denying oneself, following Christ, and being a man the Lord is delighted with are the only qualifiers that can guarantee the designation of a Good Man. *"Teach me, O Lord, to follow every one of your principles. Give me understanding and I will obey your law; I will put it into practice with all my heart. Make me walk along the path of your commands, for that is where my happiness is found."* Psalm 119: 33-35 (NLT)

"A Good Man"

God created all of his creatures and placed them on this
Earth.
Each one so unique and different from the moment of their
birth.
And in his image, God created beings with a soul.
People, man and woman, with a specific purpose and goal.

Each seeking their soul mates, with oneness in heart and
mind
Facing the possible reality that a good person may be hard to
find.
One must ask, "What sets the good man from the others so
far apart?"
He is connected to his God and mate with his soul and his
heart.

A good man follows the path and the words of the
testament…
The teachings of the Bible, the rules for life, which were
heaven sent.
A man, who loves God, through his words and deeds
Always supportive of his mate when in good times or in
need.

A good man honors the Spirit by exemplifying the fruit
And leads by his actions so that others may follow suit.
And lives each day to the fullest, maintaining his spiritual
ties
Which provide the wisdom to make the good man wise.

Is truthful to God, his mate, and himself…you see
A good man, a very good man, has integrity.
Honoring each vow and true to every commitment
A devotion to honor and integrity is how his life is spent.

With more than two eyes, a perceptive mind he hath
To create the perfect vision to travel life's uncertain path.
Joining together with his spouse, walking hand and hand
Yes, this good man, ever loyal to his wife, is the good
husband.

It goes beyond the role of spouse, there is more for him to be
A good man is one when his life has passed shall leave a
legacy.
Support, patience, and love…overcoming worry and bother
A good man who unconditionally loves his children….he is
the good father.

The good man travels forward across this great and vast land
And leaves his footprints in the dirt, and deep upon the sand.
Those footsteps carry him near and far, across concrete,
grass, and board
The good man walks with his humble steps that are ordered
by the Lord.

J. Michael Coyne